KU-303-395

HOMER'S

THE ILIAD

A GRAPHIC NOVEL

BY DIEGO AGRIMBAU
& MARCELO ZAMORA

A CAPSTONE COMPANY
PUBLISHERS FOR CHILDREN

Raintree is an imprint of Capstone Global Library Limited,
a company incorporated in England and Wales having its
registered office at 264 Banbury Road, Oxford, OX2 7DY –
Registered company number: 6695582

www.raintree.co.uk
myorders@raintree.co.uk

© **Latinbooks International S.A.**, under license of
Cypres S.A. 2014. All rights reserved. This **English** edition
distributed and published by © **Capstone Global Library
Limited** 2018. No part of this publication may be reproduced
in any form or by any means (including photocopying or
storing it in any medium by electronic means and whether
or not transiently or incidentally to some other use of this
publication) without the written permission of the copyright
owner, except in accordance with the provisions of the
Copyright, Designs and Patents Act 1988 or under the
terms of a licence issued by the Copyright Licensing Agency,
Saffron House, 6–10 Kirby Street, London EC1N 8TS
(www.cla.co.uk). Applications for the copyright owner's
written permission should be addressed to the publisher.

ISBN 978 1 4747 5139 1 (paperback)

British Library Cataloguing in Publication Data
A full catalogue record for this book is available from the
British Library.

By Diego Agrimbau & Marcelo Zamora

Translated into the English language by Trusted Translations

Every effort has been made to contact copyright holders
of material reproduced in this book. Any omissions will be
rectified in subsequent printings if notice is given to the
publisher.

All the Internet addresses (URLs) given in this book were valid
at the time of going to press. However, due to the dynamic
nature of the Internet, some addresses may have changed, or
sites may have changed or ceased to exist since publication.
While the author and publisher regret any inconvenience this
may cause readers, no responsibility for any such changes can
be accepted by either the author or the publisher.

Printed and bound in United Kindom.

CONTENTS

ZEUS

APHRODITE

HECTOR

HELEN

PARIS

MENELAUS

The silence of dawn was interrupted by the thunderous voice of Priam, king of Troy.

My son! I want to see my son!

Hecuba!

Look, my love! Our child has already been born. It's a boy!

But these words were not news to the king of Troy. His daughter Cassandra, the wisest oracle in the city, had already foreseen it.

The child must be killed. Because of him, Troy will burn. I have seen it in my dreams.

Kill him before it's too late.

Cassandra was never wrong...

...and her father knew it.

Some time later, a wedding was celebrated in Olympia, between the beautiful goddess Thetis and Peleus, son of Aeacus. Only one goddess was not invited: Eris. The all-powerful Zeus did not want any trouble at the banquet.

But even though she wasn't present, Eris managed to get up to her old tricks.

And this apple? It wasn't here a minute ago.

For the most beautiful

Given what it says, obviously it's mine.

You wish! Everyone knows I am the most beautiful.

Ha! That's what you think...

Athena, Hera and Aphrodite couldn't agree, so they asked Zeus to judge.

Don't involve me in your arguments. It would be best to ask someone else. I know a shepherd who can settle this matter.

My dear husband, it is time for you to answer our question.

Which one of us is the most beautiful?

This shepherd was none other than Paris, the boy given up by his parents and raised by shepherds. He had grown up to become the most handsome man on Earth.

After performing various sacrifices and toasts in the name of the gods, the Greeks started their attack.

But soon the Trojans showed that under the orders of their grand champion, the powerful Hector, their city would not be easily conquered.

Pallas Athena, goddess of war, protected the Greeks.

Fire!

The divine and handsome Apollo protected the Trojans.

The balance between the forces of both armies could only mean one thing…

…a cruel and long war that would cause the waters of the Aegean Sea to turn red with blood.

The Greek heroes, its best men, met to discuss the will of the gods.

A new attack would happen soon.

Odysseus, the wise.

Menelaus, the outraged king.

Agamemnon, the terrible.

And Ajax, the strong.

But the most powerful man of all, the unstoppable, handsome Achilles, would not be on their side.

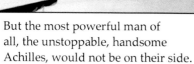

After nine years, his hard feelings towards Agamemnon's actions had not gone away.

Attack!

As they had done many times in the last nine years, the Trojan and Greek spears crossed on the battlefield.

But not everyone risked their lives on the battlefield…

SSSSWISSH!

SLACK!

CLANG!

My first husband has humiliated you, Paris.

I would ask you to return and face him, but I know you would die by his sword.

Quiet, Helen! Menelaus had help from Athena.

I will still have the opportunity to show my courage.

As the battle raged on ...

... only Achilles did not know of its cost of human life. He, whom the gods had given superhuman, invincible strength ...

The enormous shadow of the giant Sarpedon, the son of Zeus and a mortal woman, filled the Greek faces with dread.

Zeus himself filled Hector's body with superhuman strength.

AAAH!

The Greeks' fate seemed to be sealed.

It was then, within the broken Greek lines that still fought, that an old man put new life into their strength and spirits.

The future and glory of Greece is in your hands!

Take up your weapons and shields!

You heard the wise man! Attack! We win or we die!

So that was how the Greeks and Trojans, driven by the wishes of the gods, continued to fight once again.

The war was far from over yet.

Achilles asked Zeus for his friend's good fortune.

With his armour and divine protection, Patroclus would be able to fight off the Trojans' attack.

Achilles has returned! And he's coming towards Troy!

We saw his armour shine as he slashed through our men!

Indeed, Patroclus had caused the Trojans to fall back. Troy itself was his new objective.

Leave him to me, Hector. This is not the divine Achilles. It's someone else wearing his armour.

Zeus made night fall over Troy. Both sides needed to rest.

Oh, Hephaestus, god of fire. My son needs the services of your forge.

I want you to make new armour to protect his body. And the best weapons anyone has ever seen.

CLANG!

CLANG!

Hephaestus worked all night to fulfill the desires of the goddess.

Here you are, my son.

44

Following Odysseus' advice, the Greek camp began to prepare for a new battle. They gained confidence by seeing their heroes united for the same cause.

Meanwhile, on the outskirts of Troy, the enemy army was doing the same...

They say Achilles is on the battlefield once again.

I know, Paris. Today our survival will be put to the test.

A battle, the size of which has never been seen before, is nearing. Dozens of brave heroes will surely die.

Mix in with the men and defend your favourites. You are free to choose sides.

I will defend the Trojans. They need assistance from Ares, the god of war.

But they started this by stealing Helen!

Lies!

The largest battle ever fought.

TRUM TRUM TRUM

TRUM TRUM TRUM

Gods and men mixed in the final battle of the nine-year war.

SLISSSSSS!

Achilles fought and destroyed the Trojan army, bringing great honour to his reputation, which had spread all over the known world.

With the help of Achilles, the Greeks were winning. The Trojans had to fall back to the Scamander River.

We need to regroup. The troops must cross the Scamander River. Achilles will not follow us.

But, Hector ... The river will drag us to the sea... The current is as strong as a thousand bulls!

The Trojan soldiers could only choose between the sword of Achilles and the waves of the dreadful Scamander.

SHACKNNNN!

They had no other option.

Ha ha! Look at them sinking like drifting boats!

We will stain the river with the colour of their blood!

But Achilles would pay dearly for his actions...

By the gods!

48

The river god Scamander had been offended.

FOOLISH mortal! Who do you think you are, filling my river with bodies!

My name is Achilles, and I will fight against you even though you are a god!

Aaah!

Your insults will return unto you.

Scamander dumped all the bodies that Achilles had tossed into the riverbed onto the hero.

Now it was he who was fighting for his life.

49

But Achilles was not alone in this unfair fight. A powerful god came to his rescue.

Scamander! You'll regret attacking a simple mortal! My name is Hephaestus, and I've come to destroy you!

Get up, Achilles. You must continue with the battle.

But what Hector did not know was that his brother, Deiphobus, was further afield, behind Troy's walls.

That mysterious vision was nothing more than a trick of Athena…

The cruel battle had ended. It was time to heal.

What do you want to do with Hector's body, Achilles?

Leave it out there to rot... He doesn't deserve any other ritual...

Now I want to rest. Let nobody bother me.

Achilles, dear friend.

Achilles did not yet know that in his dreams he would receive an unexpected visit.

Patroclus! Forgive me, I could not save you...

Don't do it, Achilles.

Then so be it, and may our bones rest together forever.

But I will fulfill your revenge. I will bring Troy to ashes in your name!

If you try, you will die.

For a brief moment, peace between the Trojans and the Greeks was a possibility.

Paris' guilt could not be subdued. Without knowing what to do, he could only pray to his god for protection...

Great Apollo! Tell me what to do!

Draw back your bow and point it at the Greek camp. I'll do the rest.

It is the only way you can recover from this, Paris.

Paris obeyed Apollo.

FLING!

SSSSSSSSSS

Apollo did his part, guiding the arrow on its path to the hero's only weak point.

And hit the bull's-eye.

SSSSSSTHCK!

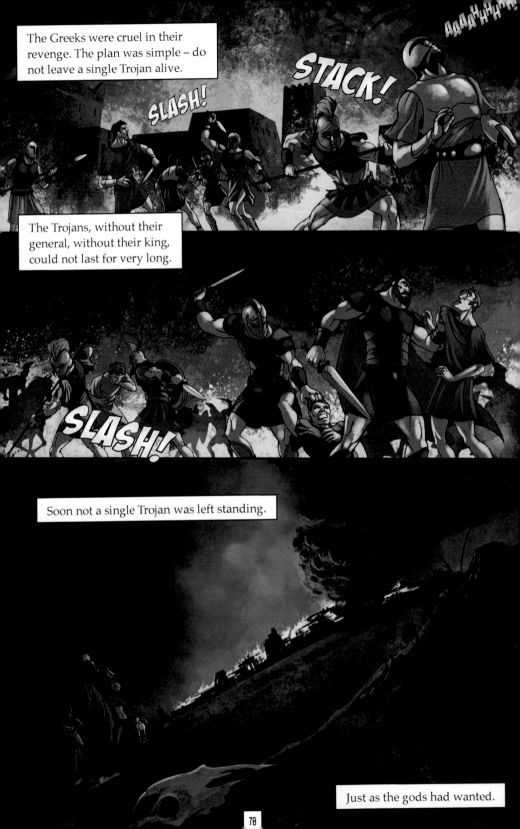

The Greeks were cruel in their revenge. The plan was simple – do not leave a single Trojan alive.

SLASH!

STACK!

AAAAHHHH!

The Trojans, without their general, without their king, could not last for very long.

SLASH!

Soon not a single Trojan was left standing.

Just as the gods had wanted.

Helen was forgiven. She could return with Menelaus.

The Greek heroes, after so much time fighting shoulder to shoulder, now set off on their return trips home. Each one with part of the loot.

The wise Odysseus could only think about returning home. But his cruelty in Troy had not gone unnoticed by the gods. He would pay for this.

Of course that ...

... is another story.

ABOUT THE AUTHOR

Homer is the name identified with a Greek poet, who lived in the eighth century
BC, to whom some of the grandest epic poems in history are attributed: *The Iliad*
and *The Odyssey*. In his biography many traditional and legendary facts are mixed
because not many precise details are known about his life, including doubts about
his historical existence. Ancient testimonies suggest he was born in the city of
Chios. One of the traditional characteristics attributed to him is blindness. In fact,
his name could come from the phrase *Ho mè horon*, which means "who does not
see". Another theory suggests that his name relates to a group of poets called
the *Homeridai*. The debate over if he is an individual author or several authors
combined still continues today.

ABOUT THE RETELLING AUTHOR AND ILLUSTRATOR

Diego Agrimbau of Buenos Aires, Argentina, has written more than a dozen
graphic novels for various publishers worldwide. He has won many prizes
among which are the Prix Utopiales 2005 for *La Burbuja de Bertold*, First Prize
Comic Planeta DeAgostini 2009 for *Planeta Extra* and the Dibujando entre
Culturas prize 2011 for *Los autómatas del Desierto*. Currently he is a collaborator
for *Fierro* magazine and writes the *Los Canillitas* comic strips for the *Tiempo
Argentino* newspaper.

Marcelo Zamora was born in Tucumán but studied in Buenos Aires, Argentina,
at the Lola Mora School of Fine Arts. He has worked as an artist and designer for
publicity agencies and as an animator for TV and film productions. He has created
illustrations for children's books and has done artistic design for video games.

GLOSSARY

champion person who fights for a cause in place of someone else

chaos total confusion; anything that throws the world out of balance, such as war

confident sure of oneself

decay break down into tiny pieces after dying

divine having to do with gods

enormous extremely large

fate events in a person's life that are determined by a supernatural power; the outcome of a situation

funeral pyre bonfire on which bodies were burned in ancient times; it was the most common funeral rite

Hades underworld in Greek mythology; the place where the souls of the dead go; also the name of the god who rules the underworld

legendary fame given to a person for accomplishing great things; someone who is legendary is the best at what he or she does

mortal human; a being who will eventually die

offend insult someone

oracle place or person that a god speaks through; in myths, gods used oracles to predict the future or to tell people how to solve problems

sacrifice offer something to a god

siege attack surrounding a city before invading it

WARS AND GODS

In the story of *The Iliad* we see various gods acting with or against the heroes. The idea of gods, or divinities, in ancient Greece was very different from that which we have nowadays. For Ancient Greeks, gods were immortal and had the power to influence humans, but they had the same traits, such as vanity and jealousy, as the mortals. Some of the most important gods who appear in this story are Zeus, Aphrodite, Athena and Apollo.

Zeus was the most important of all gods in Greek mythology. He was the one who ruled all gods and humans, and his domain was all of heaven and Earth. Zeus was the son of the titans Cronus and Rhea, against whom he headed a rebellion to take their power. He was the father of gods and humans alike. His mortal sons were demigods and were some of the greatest heroes of Greek mythology, such as Hercules, Perseus and Sarpedon, among others. In Roman mythology his equivalent was Jupiter.

Aphrodite was the goddess of love and beauty. According to the ancient myths, Aphrodite was born of the sea as an adult, but in *The Iliad* Homer said she was the daughter of Dione, an oracular goddess. She was married to Ares, the god of war, and their son is also the god of love, Eros, better known by his name in Roman mythology, Cupid. In Roman mythology, Aphrodite was known as Venus.

Athena was the goddess of wisdom and one of the most important divinities of Greek mythology. The myths say that she was the favourite child of Zeus, born as an adult from his forehead already holding weapons. Some believe it was Hephaestus who opened Zeus' head with an axe so the goddess could be born. Athena was the goddess of protection for the most important city in Greece – Athens. In Roman mythology her equivalent was Minerva.

Apollo was a multifaceted god, meaning that he gave protection to a great variety of objects and professions. Perhaps his most important and well-known identifier is that he was the god of the Sun. Like Athena, he was the son of Zeus, but in *The Iliad* he appeared to protect Troy, opposing Athena. In Roman mythology his equivalent was Phoebus.

Other important gods in the Greek culture were Artemis, Poseidon, Hades, Hermes, Ares, Hera, Hephaestus, Dionysus and Demeter.

Even though we know the traditional story of the Trojan War, in the pages of *The Iliad* the story ends the moment when Achilles brings Hector's body to Priam. The strategy of the Trojan Horse, which ended the war, can be found in the first pages of *The Aeneid*, an epic by the Roman poet Virgil. Similarly, the beginning, with the discord among the goddesses over the golden apple and the start of the war, does not appear in the original poem. In this adaptation these events were included as a prologue and an epilogue, as they provide a complete story and show the origin and destiny of the various characters involved.

DISCUSSION
QUESTIONS

1. Who do you think was to blame for the Trojan War? Paris, Helen, the gods or someone else? Explain your response.

2. Which heroes in the Trojan War do you think were the most important? Use examples from the story to explain your answer.

3. At the end of the story, Helen helps the Greeks enter the city. Do you think this was a good idea? Why do you think she did this?

4. In ancient times, people believed that prophecies of the oracles were the will of the gods and that the destiny they willed would happen no matter what. How do you think this was shown in the story of the Trojan War?

WRITING
PROMPTS

1. Between the beginning and the end of the Trojan War, nine years passed. Write a one-page story about one of the battles that happened during this time.

2. Before leaving with Helen, Paris spent several days in the palace with Menelaus. How might his days there have been spent? What could he have done? How might he have met Helen? Write a diary entry from Paris' perspective that answers some of these questions.

3. Imagine that you are a soldier in one of the two armies. Write a letter home explaining the experiences you have had in the war.

4. What do you think Paris' life as a shepherd may have been like before learning he was the prince of Troy? Write a couple of paragraphs about this.

THE ILIAD AND FILM

One of the first films about this story was released in 1956, but it centred on Helen and told the story from the side of the Trojans. This was *Helen of Troy*, filmed during the golden age of cinema in Italy. Some of the battle scenes in this film were used years later in the movie *Jason and the Argonauts*.

In 1961, *The Trojan War* was filmed. In this case the story was centred on Aeneas, a Trojan prince not present in *The Iliad*, but who is an important character in epic poetry. Aeneas is the protagonist in *The Aeneid*, the great epic poem by Virgil. The story tells of the hero's journey from the destroyed Troy to the shores of present-day Italy, where his descendants were the founders of Rome.

Recently, in 2004, a new version of the story hit the screen. This movie was called *Troy*, and it featured the renowned actor Brad Pitt in the role of Achilles. In this version, the story underwent many changes. For example, the war was reduced to no more than fifty days, no gods intervened and Achilles died after entering Troy in the horse. At the end of the film, Aeneas escapes from Troy, a clear reference to *The Aeneid*. Ironically, Brad Pitt suffered an injury to his Achilles tendon during filming.

READ THEM ALL!

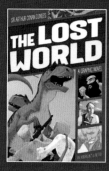

SIR ARTHUR CONAN DOYLE'S
THE LOST WORLD
A GRAPHIC NOVEL

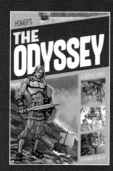

HOMER'S
THE ODYSSEY
A GRAPHIC NOVEL

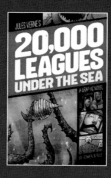

JULES VERNE'S
20,000 LEAGUES UNDER THE SEA
A GRAPHIC NOVEL

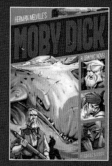

HERMAN MELVILLE'S
MOBY DICK
A GRAPHIC NOVEL

ROBIN HOOD
A GRAPHIC NOVEL

ARTHUR CONAN DOYLE'S
THE HOUND OF THE BASKERVILLES
A GRAPHIC NOVEL

MARY SHELLEY'S
FRANKENSTEIN
A GRAPHIC NOVEL

ROBERT LOUIS STEVENSON'S
TREASURE ISLAND
A GRAPHIC NOVEL

CHARLES DICKENS'S
A CHRISTMAS CAROL
A GRAPHIC NOVEL

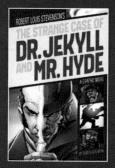

ROBERT LOUIS STEVENSON'S
THE STRANGE CASE OF DR. JEKYLL AND MR. HYDE
A GRAPHIC NOVEL

VICTOR HUGO'S
THE HUNCHBACK OF NOTRE DAME
A GRAPHIC NOVEL

BRAM STOKER'S
DRACULA
A GRAPHIC NOVEL

JULES VERNE'S
AROUND THE WORLD IN 80 DAYS
A GRAPHIC NOVEL

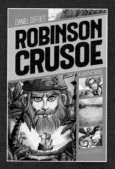

DANIEL DEFOE'S
ROBINSON CRUSOE
A GRAPHIC NOVEL

JULES VERNE'S
JOURNEY TO THE CENTER OF THE EARTH
A GRAPHIC NOVEL

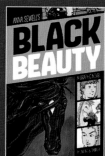

ANNA SEWELL'S
BLACK BEAUTY
A GRAPHIC NOVEL

JOHANN DAVID WYSS

THE SWISS FAMILY
ROBINSON

A GRAPHIC NOVEL

KING ARTHUR
AND THE KNIGHTS OF THE
ROUND TABLE

A GRAPHIC NOVEL

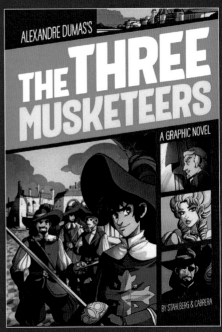

ALEXANDRE DUMAS'S

THE **THREE**
MUSKETEERS

A GRAPHIC NOVEL

BY STAHLBERG & CABRERA

PERSEUS AND
MEDUSA

A GRAPHIC NOVEL

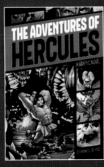

THE ADVENTURES OF
HERCULES

A GRAPHIC NOVEL

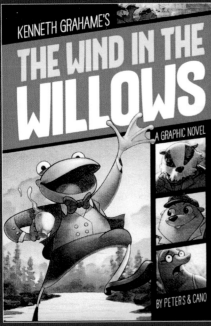

KENNETH GRAHAME'S

THE WIND IN THE
WILLOWS

A GRAPHIC NOVEL

BY PETERS & CANO

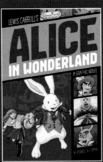

LEWIS CARROLL'S

ALICE
IN WONDERLAND

A GRAPHIC NOVEL

JONATHAN SWIFT'S

GULLIVER'S
TRAVELS

A GRAPHIC NOVEL

MARK TWAIN'S

THE ADVENTURES OF
TOM SAWYER

A GRAPHIC NOVEL

J.M. BARRIE'S

PETER PAN

A GRAPHIC NOVEL

BY HELENA & CANO

ONLY FROM RAINTREE BOOKS!